DAYS T... WORLD

THE ... OF N... M...A

11 FEBRUARY 1990

Liz Gogerly

HODDER Wayland

an imprint of Hodder Children's Books

DAYS THAT SHOOK THE WORLD

Produced by Monkey Puzzle Media Ltd
Gissing's Farm, Fressingfield
Suffolk IP21 5SH, UK

First published in 2003 by Hodder Wayland
An imprint of Hodder Children's Books
Text copyright © 2003 Hodder Wayland
Volume copyright © 2003 Hodder Wayland

Series Concept:	Liz Gogerly
Commissioning Editor:	Jane Tyler
Editor:	Patience Coster
Picture Researcher:	Lynda Lines
Design:	Jane Hawkins
Consultant:	Michael Rawcliffe
Map artwork:	Michael Posen

Cover picture: Nelson Mandela walks to freedom on 11 February 1990.

Title page picture: Mandela on the campaign trail during the 1994 elections, after which
he became South Africa's first black president.

We are grateful to the following for permission to reproduce photographs:
AKG London 12; Associated Press 17 bottom (Jurgern Schadeburg), 31 (Tomkins), 32
(David Van-Gur); Camera Press 14, 15 (S. Simon), 24, 30; Corbis front cover (Sygma), 6
top (Charles O'Rear), 7 (David Turnley), 33 (Nigel Farrow/Assignments Photographers),
35 (Louise Gubb/Saba), 36 (Sygma), 37 (Louise Gubb/Saba); Hulton Archive 21 (Bert
Hardy), 25 (Mary Benson); Popperfoto 10, 13 (Reuters), 16, 22 top (Reuters), 22 bottom,
39, 41 top (Reuters); Press Association 43 (EPA); Rex Features 3 (Markus Zeffler), 8
(Markus Zeffler), 19 top (Sipa), 34 (Mark Peters/Sipa), 38 top (Juhan Kuus/Sipa), 40
(Markus Zeffler), 42 (Stuart Clarke); Topham Picturepoint 11, 18, 19 bottom, 27, 38
bottom (ImageWorks), 41 bottom (Louise Gubb/ImageWorks); UWC-Robben Island
Mayibuye Archives 9, 17 top, 20, 23, 26, 28 both, 29.

Printed in Hong Kong by Wing King Tong

British Library Cataloguing in Publication Data
Gogerly, Liz
The freeing of Nelson Mandela. - (Days that shook the world)
1.Mandela, Nelson, 1918- - Imprisonment - Juvenile literature
2.Apartheid - South Africa - Juvenile literature
3.South Africa - History - 1961– - Juvenile literature
I.Title
968'.064'092

ISBN 07502 4409 7

Hodder Children's Books
A division of Hodder Headline Limited
338 Euston Road, London NW1 3BH

A Day to Remember

> " In a world that had become cynical and tired of politicians, to people bored with the tawdry promise of an ever-better tomorrow, Nelson Mandela represented moral certainty and personal dignity. "
>
> *BBC journalist and correspondent for South Africa, George Alagiah, writing about the impact of Nelson Mandela's release.*

In 1994 Nelson Mandela became the first black president of South Africa. In the same year he revisited Robben Island as a free man. He is shown here in the two-metre-wide cell where he was held captive for many years.

on 11 February 1990, the world was waiting. When Mandela took his first steps out of the gates of Victor Verster prison, a host of media photographers caught the dignity and defiance of a man who had refused to give up the crusade for freedom.

For many people the release of Nelson Mandela was one of the most memorable events of the twentieth century. It represented the freeing of all black South Africans from the oppression of apartheid. It also represented the triumph of one remarkable man over the injustice of white supremacy.

The evening before he left prison, Mandela was thoughtful and subdued. His excitement at being released was mixed with sadness at having to say goodbye to the prison officers and guards with whom he had become friendly. One of Mandela's many admirable characteristics is his ability to look beyond skin colour and political differences when forming friendships. His release would mark the beginning of the next chapter in his life. At nearly seventy-two years of age – a time of life when most people are retired – he was not just stepping back into public life, but shouldering the burden of his country's future.

On the morning of 11 February, thousands of news reporters and millions of people waited expectantly for Mandela's release. But he went about his routine much the same as usual. He awoke at 4.30 am and did his exercises, then washed and ate breakfast. As the sun rose in the cloudless skies over Cape Town, he packed his books and papers. Though he had few possessions, his time in prison had enriched his mind. He had spent years reading and studying the history of his country and other nations. Through his experience of imprisonment he had acquired the wisdom and strength to tackle the difficulties that lay ahead. In prison, Mandela had become a hero to the people of South Africa. Was the free man going to live up to their expectations?

Mandela visits the Great Palace in the Transkei where he lived with his uncle, Chief Jongintaba, when he was nine.

O N 10 MAY 1994, NELSON MANDELA was elected as the first black president of the republic of South Africa. As president, he was respected throughout the world. And, although he retired from office in 1999 he is still regarded as a powerful voice in international politics. Many words sum up his personality – dignified, humorous, shy, courageous, gentle, humble, vain and ruthless. This blend of characteristics is partly the result of his years as a freedom fighter and in prison, but it is also the result of his childhood.

Mandela has been described as a combination of African aristocrat and English gentleman. When he

was born, on 18 July 1918, he was called Rolihlahla, which means 'troublemaker' in the Xhosa language. As the son of the chief of the Thembu people, Mandela was born into African royalty. But his childhood was not privileged by Western standards. Mandela grew up in a cluster of mud huts in the small village of Qunu in the rolling countryside of the Transkei, South Africa. He was raised by his mother and lived a life based upon the simple customs and rituals of the Thembu people.

Mandela was a clever child and at the age of seven became the first person in his family to go to school. The school he attended had been founded by British

European settlers were ruthlessly carving up the land in South Africa. In 1867, diamonds were discovered on the Orange River. Four years later, the British founded the town of Kimberley which soon became the centre of the diamond industry. The British met with fierce opposition from the Boers and the Zulus. In 1877 the British annexed the Transvaal and two years later attempted to invade Zululand. Despite heavy losses, the British crushed the mighty Zulus. But in 1881 the Boers defeated the British and regained independence in the Transvaal. So ended the first Boer War in which more than 9,000 British soldiers were killed. In the second Boer War of 1899-1902, the British defeated the Boers again, but it was a long, hard war in which many more lives were lost on both sides.

As a boy, Mandela enjoyed listening to the stories about brave Xhosa warriors and the great battles of the past. But years later in his cell at Robben Island, he read about the history of the European colonists and sought to understand the struggle between the races in his country.

A World Apart

"I came across few whites as a boy at Qunu. The local magistrate, of course, was white, as was the nearest shopkeeper. Occasionally white travellers or policemen passed through our area. These whites appeared as grand as gods to me, and I was aware that they were to be treated with a mixture of fear and respect. But their role in my life was a distant one, and I thought little if at all about the white man in general or relations between my own people and these curious and remote figures."

From Long Walk to Freedom *by Nelson Mandela.*

Zulu spears bring down British soldiers in a battle near Ladysmith (now part of KwaZulu-Natal) in May 1879 during the British-Zulu War. But by July 1879 the British had won the war.

This photo from 1900 shows a black servant pulling a rickshaw. With well-paid jobs barred to them, many black South Africans worked as servants for white colonists.

THE END OF THE SECOND BOER WAR DID NOT bring peace. The Boers, who were also known as Afrikaaners, were deeply resentful of British rule. Meanwhile, many black Africans who had fought for the British Empire against the Boers were badly let down when the British failed to give them the vote. In 1910 the British government unified the Cape Colony, Natal, Transvaal and the Orange Free State to form the Union of South Africa. But voting rights were still denied to non-whites.

In 1911 the new prime minister of South Africa, the Afrikaaner Louis Botha, passed the Mines and Works Acts. These laws created a 'colour bar' in employment. This meant that blacks were banned from most well-paid jobs and forced to do low-paid,

unskilled work instead. Then, in 1913, the Native Land Act was passed, which meant that black Africans were not allowed to buy land from or sell it to white people. The act allocated 92.7 per cent of the land to the country's white population (1.5 million people). The majority black population (5.5 million) was given the remaining 7.3 per cent of the land.

In 1914 South African soldiers fought for the British Empire in the First World War. Once again, black soldiers fought for the King of England but were still not granted the vote when the war ended in 1918. Nelson Mandela was raised in a tradition where the voice of every man is heard, but he was born at a time when only white men could vote.

A mineworker in 1940. Despite the risks of working deep underground, miners wore no safety gear and worked long shifts for low wages.

During the following decades, more laws and government rulings reduced the rights of black Africans. In 1923, the Native Urban Areas Act was passed. It resulted in separate areas being created to house black people in the towns. Then, in 1924, General Hertzog, a veteran from the Boer War, became prime minister. He recommended independence from the British Empire and aimed to increase racial segregation. Although Hertzog did not win independence from Britain (this was achieved in 1961), he successfully championed the cause of Afrikaaner 'poor whites'. Under Hertzog, many black Africans were sacked so that the poor whites could have their jobs.

In 1939 South Africans fought on the British side in the Second World War. Factories and industries sprang up to support the war effort. There were more jobs in the towns and cities and many black Africans moved there in search of work. In 1940, Nelson Mandela headed for Johannesburg. He wanted to qualify as a lawyer but initially found a job as a night watchman for a gold mine. With his pockets jangling with money for the first time, he did not ask himself why the son of a chief, with a good education, could not find a better job. It took a few years, and many hard knocks, before the proud young man questioned what was going on in his country.

Political Beginnings

"It was one of the first mixed gatherings I had ever attended, and I was far more of an observer than a participant. I felt extremely shy, wary of committing a faux pas [saying the wrong thing], and unequipped to participate in the high-flown and rapid-fire conversations. My thoughts seemed undeveloped by comparison to the sophisticated dialogue around me."

Nelson Mandela remembering some of the first political meetings he attended in Johannesburg in the early 1940s.

A FEW WEEKS AFTER ARRIVING IN JOHANNESBURG Mandela met an estate agent named Walter Sisulu (see box opposite). Sisulu introduced him to Lazar Sidelsky, a Jewish lawyer. Sidelsky was so impressed with Mandela that he took him on as a trainee lawyer. By 1943 Mandela had completed his college degree at Fort Hare through a correspondence course. In 1944 he began studying law part-time at the University of Witwatersrand.

With his immaculate suits and 'princely' air, Mandela looked the part of a young professional, but that did not mean his life was easy. When Mandela started as a trainee, Sidelsky gave him one of his old suits to wear because Mandela could not afford to buy one. For a while Mandela lived in Alexandra, a black township known as the 'Dark City' because there was no electricity. Money was so tight that he often walked the 20 kilometres to work to avoid paying the bus fare. At university he suffered racist abuse from some of the white students.

To work against this kind of racist abuse, Mandela joined an organization called the African National Congress (ANC). Formed in 1912 by a group of black African intellectuals, the ANC fought for freedom and rights for Africans. The early members of the ANC hoped they could overturn some of the laws and changes to their country by petitioning the government. However, they had failed to prevent the race laws that were steadily being introduced.

When Mandela joined the ANC in 1943 a new phase in the struggle for liberation was set to begin. At the home of Walter Sisulu, Mandela met young men such as Anton Lembede. At this time the ANC was pressing for more rights for black people. Lembede believed that blacks should not just have more rights but that they should govern South Africa. In 1944 he founded the ANC Youth League to coordinate demonstrations against the white government. Mandela was elected to the committee, along with Walter Sisulu and another ex-Fort Hare student, Oliver Tambo.

The South African government's pass laws restricted the movement of non-whites, who were forced to carry a passbook (form of identification) wherever they went. In this photograph from the 1920s, people are protesting against the pass laws.

Walter Sisulu (1912–2003)

When Nelson Mandela first arrived in Johannesburg he believed that any African who wanted to succeed in business needed to have a degree. In Walter Sisulu he found a man without a university education who was nevertheless rising through the ranks of the ANC. Sisulu was born in the Transkei and had worked as a labourer before moving to Johannesburg where he became a successful estate agent. He joined the ANC in 1940, and became treasurer of the Youth League in 1944. By 1949 he was secretary-general of the ANC but was forced to resign his post in 1954 because he was banned by the government. He continued to work underground, but was arrested in 1963 and found guilty of treason. During his long prison sentence on Robben Island he studied for a degree in art history and anthropology (the study of human society and custom). He was released from prison in 1989, and in 1991 was elected deputy president of the ANC.

The Second World War generated jobs for thousands of black Africans, many of whom had joined trade unions to protect their interests. In 1946, 70,000 black miners went on strike in protest against low wages. Police violence repressed the strike. Twelve of the strikers were killed, union leaders were thrown in jail, and the miners were forced back to work. In the same year the government passed the Asiatic Land Tenure Act, which restricted the areas in which people from India could live and work. The Indian community in South Africa responded with mass demonstrations. During the following two years 2,000 Indian protestors were sent to jail. These events had a profound effect on Mandela. He was angry, but he had discovered a form of passive resistance (non-violent protest) that the ANC could copy.

As well as fighting for black rights, Mandela trained as a boxer. Most evenings he spent more than an hour in the gym.

Under apartheid, whites and non-whites used different facilities, such as taxis, public lavatories, beaches and even park benches. The best facilities were reserved for the use of whites only.

DR DANIEL MALAN WAS A FANATICAL AFRIKAANER who had served under General Hertzog. In 1934 he broke away from the government to form the National Party. In the general election of 1948 the National Party began its campaign with the slogan: 'Our own people, our own language, our own land'. The nationalists intended to break away from British rule and introduce apartheid to South Africa. Malan planned to separate the races of South Africa by housing them in different areas, and making them use separate facilities. He would impose these changes by making them the law. When the nationalists won the election by a large majority, Mandela was horrified: 'we knew that our land would henceforth be a place of tension and strife,' he said.

Within five years South Africa was transformed. In 1949, the Prohibition of Mixed Marriages Act made it illegal for people of different races to marry one another. In the following year, the Immorality Act made it illegal for people from different races to have sexual relations with each other. In the Population Registration Act of 1950, South Africans were divided into White, 'Coloured' (people of mixed race), Indian and African racial groups. The Group Area Act of 1950 then made it law that the different races should live in separate areas. In urban areas, Indian and Coloured people were forced to move out of the newly formed 'white areas'. African areas within the city limits were demolished and townships were built on the outskirts of the towns.

In 1952 new pass laws meant that non-whites had to carry passes with them at all times. Being caught without a pass could now mean being arrested or beaten up by the police. In 1953 the Separate Amenities Act divided all public facilities, including beaches, restaurants and cinemas, into 'white only', 'Coloured zones', 'Asian zones' and 'black zones'. In the same year, all missionary-run schools were closed and 'native schools' were opened. These schools were for non-white children only, and the facilities and teaching were of a lower standard than in white-only schools. School curricula were designed to teach non-white children that they were racially inferior.

While the government imposed these drastic policies, Mandela was rising through the ranks of the ANC. In 1950 he was elected president of the Youth League. His personal life had moved on, too. In 1944 he had married a nurse called Evelyn Mase. By the early 1950s they had two young sons and a daughter and had set up home in the township of Orlando in Johannesburg. Although they had no electricity and only an outside toilet, Mandela was proud of his home. But increasingly his political activities and his work at the law practice that he had set up with his partner, Oliver Tambo, would take him further away from his family.

Oliver Tambo (1917–93)

Tambo was the son of a farmer from the Transkei. When Mandela first met him at Fort Hare, he was impressed by Tambo's intelligence and ability to take control of a debate. The two men did not meet again until the 1940s when they were both members of the ANC. Tambo went on to become vice-president of the Youth League, and in 1952 became Mandela's partner in the law firm, 'Mandela and Tambo'. He was elected deputy president of the ANC in 1958, and when the ANC was banned in 1960 he formed a branch of it in London. In 1967 he became acting president of the ANC, then president in 1977 and acting chairman in 1991. When Oliver Tambo died of a stroke in 1993, Mandela was devastated at the loss of one of his closest friends.

Mandela with his first wife Evelyn Mase, in 1944.

This photograph from 1952 shows Mandela in the offices of the Johannesburg law firm 'Mandela and Tambo'.

I N INDIA DURING THE 1930S, MAHATMA GANDHI (1869-1948) had led a protest movement against British rule. Gandhi had practised as a lawyer in South Africa between 1898 and 1914. In India he brought the British to the negotiating table by practising non-violent protest. By attending marches, deliberately disobeying laws and incurring arrest and imprisonment, he helped to bring about Indian independence from British rule in August 1947.

A Moment in Time

In India on 12 March 1930, Mohandas Gandhi (known as 'Mahatma' or 'Great Soul') begins a 320-kilometre march from Ahmedabad to the coast on the Gulf of Cambay, near Jalalpur. Although he is frail and elderly, he undertakes the long journey on foot to collect a small piece of salt from the sea. This simple gesture symbolizes his defiance of British rule in India. The British government has established a monopoly on the production of salt. By collecting a small amount of the naturally occurring mineral, Gandhi hopes to be arrested. He tells the 79 followers who have accompanied him on his march to be prepared 'for the worst, even death, for defiance of the salt tax.'

During the 1950s the ANC in South Africa collaborated with the South African Indian Congress (SAIC). Together they masterminded a campaign of non-violent mass protest similar to that staged in India by Gandhi and his followers.

The Defiance Campaign began on 26 June 1951. On this day, thirty-three protestors entered the railway station at Port Elizabeth through the 'Whites Only' entrance. Later that day, Walter Sisulu led a group of protestors who did not possess proper passbooks into a black township. They were all arrested. That evening, Mandela was also arrested and thrown into jail for a few days.

As the protestors were transported to jail they were in high spirits and sang the rousing words of 'Nkosi Sikelel' iAfrika' ('God Bless Africa'). When they reached the prison they chanted, 'Hey, Malan! Open the jail doors. We want to enter.' On the first day of the Defiance Campaign, 250 people were arrested for violating race laws. During the next five months, a further 8,500 people were imprisoned for staging similar protests.

SLEGS BLANKES.
EUROPEANS ONLY.

Black protestors deliberately break the law by crowding into the carriage of a 'whites-only' train during the Defiance Campaign in 1952.

More defiance: Mandela makes a show of burning his passbook in 1960.

The campaign had the desired effect of boosting membership of the ANC and threatening the South African government. Unfortunately, it also prompted the government to make new laws to tackle future rebellions. The passing of the Public Safety Act in 1953 meant that the government had the power to declare martial law and detain people without trial. The Criminal Laws Amendment Act meant that protestors could receive corporal punishment. The government also issued banning orders on anybody they considered a threat to national security. Mandela called banning 'a kind of walking imprisonment', because it prevented an individual from taking part in political activity or attending gatherings of any kind, and it seriously restricted a person's movements around the country. Over the next decade, Mandela would be arrested and banned countless times, and his political activities would be driven further and further underground.

By the end of 1952, Mandela had devised the M plan – a secret network of ANC groups. By the end of 1953, he was also slowly moving towards another way of fighting the government. During the brief lifting of a ban against him, he spoke to a crowd in Sophiatown near Johannesburg. At one point he began singing: 'There are the enemies [gesturing to the police presence]… let us take our weapons and attack them.' It was the first time he had recommended using violence in the struggle.

Supporters of the ANC flock to shake hands with Mandela. By 1953 Mandela was talking about using violence to bring down the apartheid regime.

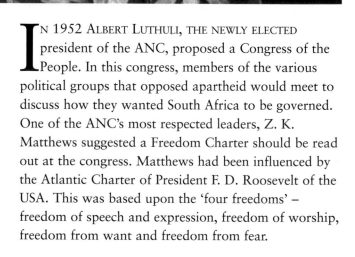

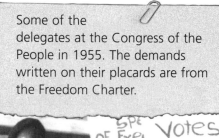
Some of the delegates at the Congress of the People in 1955. The demands written on their placards are from the Freedom Charter.

From the Freedom Charter...

" We, the people of South Africa, declare for all our country and the world to know:

'That South Africa belongs to all who live in it, black and white, and that no government can justly claim authority unless it is based on the will of the people;

'That our people have been robbed of their birthright to land, liberty and peace by a form of government founded on injustice and inequality;

'That our country will never be prosperous or free until all our people live in brotherhood, enjoying equal rights and opportunities;

'These freedoms we will fight for, side by side, throughout our lives, until we have won our liberty. "

IN 1952 ALBERT LUTHULI, THE NEWLY ELECTED president of the ANC, proposed a Congress of the People. In this congress, members of the various political groups that opposed apartheid would meet to discuss how they wanted South Africa to be governed. One of the ANC's most respected leaders, Z. K. Matthews suggested a Freedom Charter should be read out at the congress. Matthews had been influenced by the Atlantic Charter of President F. D. Roosevelt of the USA. This was based upon the 'four freedoms' – freedom of speech and expression, freedom of worship, freedom from want and freedom from fear.

Participating organizations invited their followers to make recommendations for the charter. Suggestions flooded in from sports clubs, church groups, farm workers, women and children. Some were submitted on scraps of paper or on the back of cigarette packets. The most common request was for one-person, one-

In South Africa during the 1950s black people lived in grinding poverty. The Congress of the People gave them the opportunity to speak out against the conditions in which they lived.

vote. When Mandela was asked to review the charter he was moved by what he saw: 'It was humbling to see how the suggestions of ordinary people were often far ahead of those of the leaders.'

On 25 and 26 June 1955, the Congress of the People finally went ahead at Kliptown, a village near Johannesburg. Mandela was under a ban so he disguised himself and watched the event from the crowd. The police had set up road blocks, but despite this more than 3,000 people, including 2,300 black Africans, 230 Indians, 230 'Coloured' people and 112 whites managed to gather to hear the Freedom Charter being read out. On the first day the charter was read out in English, Xhosa and Sesotho (another language of South Africa). As each clause was read out, the crowd gave their approval by shouting 'Afrika!'. Mandela described the atmosphere as 'both serious and festive', but on the second day terror

reigned when armed police stormed the stage. One of the policemen grabbed the microphone and told the crowd that treason was suspected and no one should leave without permission. Mandela managed to escape, but the rest of the crowd had to give their names for police records. This meant that if they were found at another political gathering then they could be arrested and banned.

The Congress of the People had been broken up, but the Freedom Charter was to become the liberation struggle's manifesto. In December 1956, Mandela was arrested for his alleged part in the creation of the charter. The government claimed that it was a communist document. As a result, 156 people, including Nelson Mandela, Oliver Tambo and Walter Sisulu, were arrested under the Suppression of Communism Act (a law that had been passed in 1950 to prevent communist activity in South Africa). They were charged with treason.

IN DECEMBER 1956, MANDELA'S WIFE EVELYN AND his three children watched as he was led away by white policemen. At Christmas he was let out on bail, but he returned to an empty home. For years Evelyn had begged him to make a choice between his family and his political activities. In the early days Mandela had tried to be a good father, but juggling work commitments and attending ANC meetings meant leaving the house early in the morning and returning late at night. When his first son, Thembi, was five he had asked his mother: 'Where does Daddy live?'

Mandela married his second wife, Winnie Nomzamo Madikizela, in June 1958.

Mandela and Evelyn finally divorced in 1958. By this time, Mandela had fallen in love with a beautiful young social worker called Winnie Nomzamo Madikizela. They were married in June 1958 and, in the following year, Winnie gave birth to their first daughter, Zenani. In 1960 they had another daughter, Zindzi. But the midnight raids by the police and the absences from home continued to be as much a part of Mandela's second family life as they had been of his first.

As Mandela built his new life with Winnie, the trial for treason that had begun when he was arrested in 1956 dragged on. As the Treason Trial, as it became known, continued, events in South Africa became more violent. The country was in the ever-tightening grip of white control. On 21 March 1960 the anti-apartheid group, the Pan Africanist Congress (PAC) organized a protest against pass laws in Sharpeville, a township 56 kilometres south of Johannesburg. A peaceful crowd of about 15,000 protestors converged on the police station. A line of 75 policemen attempted to push them back but, when the protestors threw stones, the police opened fire on them. Sixty-nine people were killed and hundreds more were injured.

News reporters described the scene as 'a world war battlefield' and photographs of the massacre were relayed around the world. Criticism from abroad and attempts by the UN Security Council to persuade the South African government to introduce equality for all

Photographs like this, of dead people lying in the streets of Sharpeville, alerted the world to the mounting problems in South Africa.

its peoples had no effect. The police commander in Sharpeville tried to justify his actions: 'If they [protestors] do these things, they must learn the hard way.' His attitude was echoed by the South African government, which blamed troublemakers for the unrest. On 28 March, protests in Cape Town turned into riots, and the South African government declared a State of Emergency, outlawing all black political organizations, including the ANC.

A few days later, Mandela was arrested and taken back to prison. He stayed there until the State of Emergency was lifted in August. The Treason Trial continued until 29 March 1961. Mandela conducted his own defence during the trial and impressed his followers with his eloquence and natural leadership qualities. He was found not guilty of treason, but he knew that it would only be a matter of time before the police arrested him again.

A photo montage of the 156 people arrested for treason in 1956. Mandela stands in the third row from the front, fifth from the right.

Mandela on Trial

❝ *We demand universal adult franchise [voting rights] and we are prepared to exert economic pressure to attain our demands. We will launch defiance campaigns, stay-at-homes, either singly or together, until the Government should say, 'Gentleman, we cannot have this state of affairs…. Let's talk.' In my own view I would say, 'Yes, let us talk,' and the Government would say, 'We think that the Europeans at present are not ready for a type of government where they might be dominated by non-Europeans. We think we should give you 60 seats. The African population to elect 60 Africans to represent them in Parliament. We will leave the matter over for five years and we will review it at the end of five years.' In my view, that would be a victory, My Lords; we would have taken a significant step towards the attainment of universal adult suffrage [voting rights] for Africans, and we would then for the five years say that we will suspend civil disobedience.* **❞**

Nelson Mandela speaking in his own defence during the Treason Trial, 1961.

Between 1955 and 1960, the black residents of Sophiatown near Johannesburg were evicted and relocated, mostly to the township of Soweto. Mandela campaigned against the forced removal of his people from one area to another.

A Moment in Time

AFTER THE TREASON TRIAL MANDELA WENT underground completely. For the rest of 1961 he lived the life of a fugitive, adopting different disguises and moving from one safe house to another. Mandela was always known for his smart suits, but now he dressed as a gardener, labourer or chauffeur. These were the kind of jobs taken by black people who worked in white-only areas. By disguising himself in this way he could hide in white suburbs which were less likely to be searched by the police than the black areas. The tall, proud man with the commanding presence was forced to live quietly and stay indoors during the day. He appeared at secret meetings of the ANC throughout South Africa. Liberal newspapers depicted him as a hero figure.

Mandela is staying with a white friend. His leaders tell him it's a good idea to hide out in a white-only area because the authorities would never suspect he was there. Mandela is an active man and he tells his friend that in the townships he likes to go for long runs. 'You can't do that here, man,' says his friend, 'they patrol the area and you'll be arrested!' Mandela smiles and tells him that he will go for his run. When his host wakes the next morning he is stunned to see Mandela pulling on his tracksuit. 'I'm not giving you a key to go out!' he warns him. At that, Mandela begins running on the spot. He runs on the spot for more than an hour before doing his stretches for another hour. 'That's all right, you can do this here,' says his friend. 'Yes,' answers Mandela, 'and tomorrow… you are going to join me.'

While Mandela was undercover he helped to organize the mass stay-at-home of May 1961. On the first day of the protest, thousands of people stayed away from work. Although the stay-at-home was well supported, it failed to have the necessary impact on the government. If anything, it aggravated the police and created more tension. On the second day, Mandela called the protest off. In interviews with local and foreign journalists he was in fighting spirit: 'If the government reaction is to crush by naked force our non-violent struggle, we will have to reconsider our tactics. In my mind we are closing a chapter on this question of non-violent policy.' Mandela finally convinced the ANC that he should set up a terrorist wing, to be called Umkhonto we Sizwe (Spear of the Nation) or MK.

In October 1961 Mandela moved to a permanent safe house in Rivonia, a northern suburb of Johannesburg. He managed a few secret meetings with Winnie and his daughters, but most of his time was spent planning and recruiting for MK. Mandela had no military training but the aims of MK were to stage sabotage, guerrilla warfare, terrorism and open revolution.

Although it was illegal for him to leave the country, Mandela was smuggled out of South Africa in January 1962 to visit independent African nations such as Tanzania, Ghana, Nigeria and Egypt. He met prominent African leaders like Julius Nyerere, the first president of the newly independent Tanzania. He also met up with Oliver Tambo who had left South Africa in 1960 to generate support for the ANC abroad. On the last leg of his journey he visited London, before returning to Algeria and Ethiopia for military training. After two months of learning how to make bombs and use guns, Mandela was called back to South Africa by the ANC to resume high command of the MK. He was relieved to be home, but the political situation there had become more highly charged. A new law had been passed, which meant that treason was now punishable by death.

On a visit to London in 1962, Mandela is photographed in front of some of the city's most famous landmarks, including Westminster Abbey and Big Ben.

The men in the Rivonia Trial became known as the 'Rivonia Eight'. In 1964 these men were sentenced to life imprisonment. Top row (left to right): Nelson Mandela, Walter Sisulu, Govan Mbeki, Raymond Mhlaba.

Bottom row (left to right): Elias Motsoaledi, Andrew Mlangeni, Ahmed Kathrada, Dennis Goldberg.

IN JULY 1962 THE POLICE FINALLY CAUGHT UP WITH Nelson Mandela. He was charged with leaving the country without a passport and inciting people to strike. He was given a five-year sentence at the infamous Robben Island prison. Robben Island is a narrow rock about 11 kilometres off the coast of Cape Town. When Mandela arrived there he had no idea that he would be spending so many years in that lonely place. When the guards barked out their demands he stood his ground and they left him alone. But, like the thousand other inmates, he had to do hard labour, breaking stones in a quarry.

In July 1963, less than six months into his sentence, the police raided the farmhouse in Rivonia where he had stayed as a fugitive. During their search they found Mandela's diary about his African tour and papers in his handwriting about guerrilla warfare and communism. It was just what the authorities needed to accuse him of sabotage and conspiracy to overthrow the South African government. They now had the evidence they required to charge him with high treason.

The Rivonia Trial opened in October 1963 in Pretoria. Supporters of Mandela were shocked when they saw him enter the courtroom for the first time. He appeared gaunt and broken by his short term in prison. As the trial progressed, many of Mandela's supporters were impressed by his calm, tact, diplomacy and his conviction for the struggle. 'I do not deny that I planned sabotage,' he told the court. 'We had either to accept inferiority or fight against it by violence.' Many people believed that he and Walter Sisulu would hang, but Mandela's strength of character and unwavering courage gave them heart.

Mandela gave a four-hour speech in his defence, towards the end of which he turned to the judge saying: 'I have cherished the ideal of a democratic and free society in which all persons live together in harmony with equal opportunities. It is an ideal which I hope to live for and achieve.' In a quieter voice he added: 'But if needs be, it is an ideal for which I am prepared to die.' Mandela was prepared for the death sentence and had even written a speech to read out in court if he was sentenced to hang. On 12 June 1964, as he awaited his sentence, he showed little visible emotion. When the judge gave him a life sentence Mandela turned to smile at his mother and Winnie who were there in the courtroom. But in the excitement and with the commotion there he couldn't make eye contact with, let alone say goodbye to, the most important women in his life.

Winifred Nomzamo Mandela (1934–)

Nelson Mandela met Winnie Nomzamo Madikizela in 1955. She was the first black social worker at Baragwanath Hospital in Johannesburg. Like Mandela, she came from the Transkei. Her parents were both teachers and she had done well at school. Mandela realized he had finally met his match in Winnie, who had a passionate and determined nature. When they married in 1958 it was the beginning of a relationship that would last until their separation in 1992 and divorce in 1996. During his imprisonment Mandela worried about the plight of his young wife, who struggled to support their girls and suffered from constant police harassment. 'I have often wondered whether any kind of commitment can ever be sufficient excuse for abandoning a young and inexperienced woman in a pitiless desert,' he said.

Mandela's wife, Winnie, and his mother appear to be in shock as they leave the Rivonia Trial following the verdict. After the trial Mandela never saw his mother again. She died while he was in prison.

Mandela sews clothes in the prison yard. This photograph, from the 1960s or 1970s, is one of the few taken of him during his captivity.

MANDELA CALLED HIS TIME ON ROBBEN ISLAND 'the dark years'. He lived in a tiny, squalid, damp cell with a narrow barred window that overlooked the exercise yard below. There was no running water, just a bucket for a toilet. When he lay down to sleep on the thin, straw mattress his head grazed one wall while his feet touched the other. In the winter, he shivered under the worn blankets. In the summer, he sweated under the scorching African skies as he worked in the yard crushing stones to make gravel for roads.

Each day was much the same as the previous one. Mandela was woken at 5.30 am each morning. He emptied his bucket and ate a breakfast of mealie pap, a kind of porridge made from corn. Afterwards he worked until noon when he was given lunch – more mealie pap diluted with water. After lunch he worked until 4 pm, then showered in cold sea water and had dinner – yet more mealie pap, but this time served with vegetables. At 8 pm all prisoners were told to go to sleep. This rigid routine was designed to break the spirits of the prisoners. But more damaging than physical hardship was separation from family and friends.

During the first years of Mandela's sentence, Winnie was only allowed to visit once every six months. For the precious half-hour they were allowed together they were divided by thick, glass windows. He was allowed letters from Winnie once every six months, but the joy they brought was diminished by the knowledge that he was powerless to support her in her own personal struggles. Some of the most painful moments for Mandela were not being allowed to attend the funerals of his eldest son, Thembi, and of his mother, both of whom died in the late 1960s.

Of the original 'Rivonia Eight', seven men, including Mandela, had been sent to Robben Island. Mandela took great comfort in their presence. For many years he was not allowed books or magazines. But while he worked in the yard he could exchange ideas and engage in lively political debates. In his final years of freedom, Mandela had begun to stand out as a leader, but in prison he discovered how to become a great leader. He learned to be patient, and to rise above the cruelty of his captors. Eventually, he was allowed to take a correspondence course with the University of London to gain his law degree. When he was granted access to books, he read about history and sought to understand the source of the problems in Africa. Prison life stripped him of his liberty, but it brought him wisdom and an enlightenment he might never have known had he remained a freedom fighter.

Enduring Prison Life

" The challenge for every prisoner, particularly every political prisoner, is how to survive prison intact, how to emerge from prison undiminished, how to conserve and even replenish one's beliefs.... Prison is designed to break one's spirit and destroy one's resolve. To do this, the authorities attempt to exploit every weakness, demolish every initiative, negate all signs of individuality.... It would be very hard, if not impossible, for one man alone to resist. I do not know that I could have done it had I been alone. But the authorities' greatest mistake was to keep us together, for together our determination was reinforced. **"**

Nelson Mandela in Long Walk to Freedom.

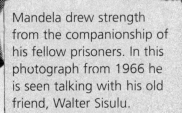

Mandela drew strength from the companionship of his fellow prisoners. In this photograph from 1966 he is seen talking with his old friend, Walter Sisulu.

MANDELA HAS OFTEN SAID THAT THE HARDSHIP he endured in prison was nothing compared with the suffering of people on the outside. In the early years at Robben Island he was not allowed newspapers, but new prisoners often smuggled in titbits of information. Eventually, Oliver Tambo and Winnie brought coded messages, and some of the wardens could be bribed to bring in newspapers. Throughout the 1960s, the news was always bleak. The government passed more laws against terrorism and established a ruthless secret service network. Tambo continued to promote the ANC from abroad, but in 1969 an uprising by ANC fighters was crushed by the South African police.

In the 1970s, black resistance took on a new identity. In 1969 Steve Biko, a black medical student from the University of Natal, formed the all-black South African Students' Organization (SASO). Biko was inspired by the civil rights campaign in the USA, particularly by the Black Power movement. He believed that black people had been made to feel inferior, and he attempted to arouse pride or 'Black Consciousness' in black South Africans. By the early 1970s, the SASO had evolved into a new party called the Black People's Convention (BPC). This was a coalition of more than 70 black organizations, and Biko was made its honorary president.

In 1973 the government restricted Biko's movements by banning him to King William's Town in the Eastern Cape, a province in southern South Africa. But he had already stirred up feeling among black youths and encouraged them to fight against the government. In 1976, when the government announced that half of all lessons in schools should be taught in Afrikaans, the children of Soweto (a black township in Johannesburg) rebelled. For them, Afrikaans was the language of white oppression. On 16 June, more than 10,000 people, many of them children wearing their school uniform, marched through the township. When the police opened fire, a thirteen-year-old boy called Hector Pietersen was killed. The children rioted, threw stones at the policemen and set fire to buildings. Their

In the 1970s Soweto's schoolchildren take to the streets in protest against overcrowded classes, lack of school equipment and the use of Afrikaans in the classroom.

anger spread to townships all over South Africa. Within three days one hundred people had been killed and thousands injured. By the end of the year, 576 people had died and 2,389 had been wounded.

Mandela only heard about the riots in August, but he managed to smuggle a statement out of prison encouraging his people to 'Unite! Mobilize! Fight On!'. In 1977, Steve Biko died while in police custody. He had been tortured and beaten, but the police claimed he had died while staging a hunger strike. By the end of the 1970s, the war against oppression had become bloody and violent and South Africa seemed to be on the verge of inter-racial civil war. On Robben Island, Mandela was relieved that his people were fighting back.

A Moment in Time

In Soweto, thousands of school children are gathered to protest against the education system. It is coming up to exam time and many of them are afraid they will fail if they have to write in Afrikaans. The marchers head towards the Orlando Stadium. There is singing and chanting. A spokesman talks to the excited children: 'Brothers and sisters, I appeal to you – keep calm. We have just received a report that the police are coming. Don't taunt them, don't do anything to them. Be cool and calm. We are not fighting.'

Soon afterwards a white policeman throws a tear-gas canister into the crowd. The children cough and splutter and start to run. A white policeman draws his revolver and fires a single shot into the crowd. For a moment there is silence, then the screaming begins. More shots are heard and some children fall to the ground. Suddenly everybody is terrified and people are running around in different directions.

At the funeral of Steve Biko, South Africans paid their last respects to a lost hero. Biko once said: 'All in all, the black man has become a shell, a shadow of man, completely defeated, drowning in his own misery.'

Freedom for All South Africans

In 1966 Prime Minister Hendrik Verwoerd was assassinated by a white parliamentary messenger. Balthazaar Johannes Vorster was elected prime minister in his place. Under Vorster's administration, the movement of Africans to the 'homelands' or 'Bantustans' was stepped up. By the 1970s, more than three million Africans had been resettled in areas of South African scrub-land. They lived in sub-standard houses with no running water or electricity and were lucky to be able to scratch a living. The white minority held on to the best land and the centres of wealth and economic power while the black majority starved.

The South African government's determination to pursue apartheid at all costs had a damaging effect on the white population too. White employers struggled to find workers and were forced to overlook some apartheid laws and employ more blacks. In 1978 the then-president, P. W. Botha relaxed some of the petty apartheid laws, including some of the pass laws, and in 1979 legalized African trade unions.

In the following years, South Africa faced industrial strikes. To add to the turmoil, countries like the USA and the EEC (European Economic Community), which had once invested heavily in the South African economy, began imposing trade sanctions to put pressure on the South African government to lift apartheid. Inflation and unemployment increased, as did the friction between political parties and the different races. Foreign entertainers and sports personalities refused to travel to South Africa. It had become a nation in torment with itself and the world.

During the 1960s, Nelson Mandela's name rarely made the newspapers at home or abroad. Then, in 1980, the Johannesburg *Sunday Post* launched the 'Free Mandela' campaign. This movement quickly gathered support in South Africa and around the world. In 1982, Mandela was moved to Pollsmoor prison in Cape Town. Conditions were slightly better here than they had been at Robben Island. Meanwhile the fight to free him stepped up. In 1984, 4,000 foreign celebrities signed a petition for Mandela's release.

By the 1980s, many black South Africans were protesting against conditions in the homelands. In the meantime their day-to-day lives remained unchanged and they struggled to survive.

By July 1985, South Africa was in the grip of worsening violence. In the townships, rival black gangs were killing one another and the South African government declared a State of Emergency. That November, the ANC presented the Harare Declaration to the government. In it they demanded the release of Mandela and other political prisoners, the lifting of the State of Emergency and the unbanning of the ANC. Botha offered freedom to Mandela on the condition that he renounce all violence. Mandela rejected the deal but in 1986, when the violence reached new heights, he entered into secret talks with the government to negotiate his freedom.

In 1988 Mandela was moved to Victor Verster prison in Paarl (see map on page 6). He was given more privileges and his own cottage. In July 1989 Mandela met with Botha for the first time. The meeting went well but Botha's health was not good, and in February 1989 F. W. de Klerk became the new president. In his inauguration speech he promised a 'new South Africa'. Mandela described de Klerk as a 'man we could do business with'. In February 1990, at the opening of Parliament, de Klerk unbanned the ANC, released political prisoners and showed his determination to lift apartheid. Several days later he announced that Mandela would also be freed.

An anti-apartheid demonstration in London in the 1980s. Meanwhile, Mandela was negotiating for his own freedom and that of his people.

The Fight for Freedom

"I am not a violent man…. It was only then, when all other forms of resistance were no longer open to us, that we turned to armed struggle. Let Botha show that he is different to Malan, Strijdom and Verwoerd. Let him renounce violence. Let him say that he will dismantle apartheid. Let him unban the people's organization, the African National Congress. Let him free all who have been imprisoned, banished or exiled for their opposition to apartheid. Let him guarantee free political activity so that people may decide who will govern them."

Part of Mandela's response to President Botha's offer of freedom in 1985. Taken from Long Walk to Freedom.

Winnie with other members of the Mandela family leaving Victor Verster prison after celebrating Mandela's seventy-first birthday in July 1989.

Early morning Members of the ANC began arriving at Nelson Mandela's cottage at Victor Verster prison to help him prepare a speech. Time seemed to being running out; there were so many things to do before 3.00 pm when he was scheduled for release. There were goodbyes to say to all the prison staff, then lunch with Winnie and other family members. Walter Sisulu and his wife Albertina were also expected.

Mid-morning Cyril Ramaphosa and Trevor Manuel of the ANC arrived at the cottage. Mandela had decided to give his speech at the Grand Parade in Cape Town. Ramaphosa and Manuel went through Mandela's speech with him, but there were other details to sort out, such as where he would spend his first night. Mandela wanted to stay in the black township in Cape Flats: 'in order to show my solidarity with the people.' Winnie, Ramaphosa and Manuel thought it would be better if he stayed

with Archbishop Desmond Tutu at his home in a white suburb of Cape Town. Nobody could imagine how Mandela's release would affect the country – perhaps there would be an uprising. If that were to be the case, he would be safer with Desmond Tutu.

Shortly after 2.00 pm Winnie, Walter Sisulu and Albertina arrived at the prison later than expected. By now there were dozens of people at Mandela's cottage. The mood was celebratory as they tucked into their final meal at the prison. Among the party were prison officers like James Gregory, who Mandela hugged and thanked for their kindness over the past two years at Victor Verster. Mandela's warmth towards the white prison guards was an indication of how he would respond when he finally left prison. In the coming months, people who feared that Mandela would be full of bitterness and hatred towards whites were surprised by his open heart and willingness to forgive.

Mandela pictured with President F. W. de Klerk after the announcement of his release. This was the first official photograph to be taken of Mandela since his imprisonment in 1964.

special request. He asked if they could film Mandela *walking* through the prison gates, rather than driving through as planned.

3.30 pm Mandela's release was behind schedule and he was impatient to leave: 'I told the members of the Reception Committee that my people had been waiting for me for 27 years and I did not want to keep them waiting for me any longer.' In his final hurry to get out, Mandela left behind his carefully prepared speech and his reading glasses.

'Welcome, Leader Mandela'

"The suspense on the day he was to be freed was tremendous. The government had lifted the ban on the ANC and other illegal organizations a week earlier. In his cottage, Mr Mandela was filling crates with books and papers – like anyone on the move. Outside the prison gates a swelling crowd of wellwishers sang freedom songs. They brought large black, green and gold ANC flags... among the T-shirt slogans 'Welcome, Leader Mandela'. Mr Mandela, a stickler for punctuality, was late emerging, but when he did so a great roar went up – 'ANC!' "

Mike Wooldridge, BBC correspondent, reporting from outside the gates of Victor Verster prison.

Outside Victor Verster prison a huge crowd of well-wishers was gathering. Television crews, reporters and photographers were waiting patiently for Mandela to make his exit. President F. W. de Klerk was not in the crowd, but he was watching the events on television from a friend's house. He had ensured that the police and army would be ready in case the situation got out of hand. His advisors knew where he was if anything should happen.

Shortly after 3.00 pm A well-known presenter from a South African television company telephoned Mandela and made a

Nelson Mandela holds on to his wife's hand as he walks through the gates of Victor Verster prison. Both he and Winnie punch the air in a victory salute.

Shortly before 4.00 pm A small motorcade finally left the cottage. Just before the gate, Mandela's car slowed down and he and Winnie stepped out and began to walk. A few minutes later they saw the huge crowd. Mandela was slightly alarmed by the scene – he had only expected the prison warders and their families to be there. He looked tense and held tightly on to Winnie's hand as he strode towards the gate. People were struck by how thin he had become and by his silver hair.

Suddenly, what seemed like thousands of cameras began clicking. Reporters shouted out questions. ANC supporters cheered and sang. Despite his bewilderment, Mandela raised his right hand into the air in the famous victory salute for the ANC. The crowd's cheers grew even louder. A few minutes later Mandela jumped back in the car. In those few precious minutes he felt filled with strength and joy: 'I felt – even at the age of 71 – that my life was beginning anew. My ten thousand days of imprisonment were at last over.'

4.14 pm After his release Mandela was driven the 56 kilometres to Cape Town. On the journey through the beautiful green Cape countryside he was struck by the number of white people who watched and waved as the motorcade drove by: 'It made me think that the South Africa I was returning to was far different from the one I left.'

Free at Last!

" Comrades and fellow South Africans, I greet you all in the name of peace, democracy and freedom for all. I stand here before you not as a prophet but as a humble servant of you, the people. Your tireless and heroic sacrifices have made it possible for me to be here today. I therefore place the remaining years of my life in your hands…

"Our struggle has reached a decisive moment: We call on our people to seize this moment, so that the process toward democracy is rapid and uninterrupted…

"We have waited too long for our freedom. We can no longer wait. Now is the time to intensify the struggle on all fronts. To relax our efforts now would be a mistake which generations to come will not be able to forgive. "

Extracts from Nelson Mandela's speech at City Hall, Cape Town, 11 February 1990.

Early evening Mandela arrived at the City Hall in Cape Town at twilight. He had left his prepared speech behind at Victor Verster so he had to remember what he wanted to say. His speech was delivered in a serious voice. He started by thanking those people throughout the world who had supported the fight against apartheid. Despite recommendations from white politicians that he should not align himself with the ANC, he went on to do just that, but he also condemned crime and violence. Some were disappointed by the delivery of his speech, but most people were impressed by his warmth and intellect and stood up to applaud him.

Soon afterwards, Mandela was driven away to Archbishop Desmond Tutu's residence at Bishopcourt. The house was filled with relatives and friends, but Mandela was most thrilled when he received a call from Oliver Tambo who was recovering from a stroke in Scandinavia. The next day, Mandela held a press conference at which he tried to soothe white fears about the future of South Africa. Mandela had wanted more time to be with his family and to visit his homeland in the Transkei. But for the next nine years duty to his country would often come before the demands of his personal life.

Mandela is renowned for his forgiveness. Here, in 1997, he is seen shaking hands with one of his former guards.

MANDELA'S RELEASE DID NOT CHANGE SOUTH Africa overnight. In fact, the situation grew worse before it improved. Between 1990 and 1994, black-on-black violence in the townships escalated, particularly between supporters of the ANC and its rival, the mainly Zulu IFP (Inkatha Freedom Party). Violence by white extremist groups added to the climate of fear. During those dreadful years, 60,000 people lost their lives. Mandela seemed to be the only hope of uniting all the warring factions and bringing peace to South Africa.

Scenes of burning and looting, and violence between rival black political groups were everyday occurrences in South Africa between 1990 and 1994.

A few days after his release, Mandela returned to his home in Soweto. While he was delighted to be back, he was shocked by the increase in crime and at the state of the township, which he believed was worse than it had been before his imprisonment. In a rally at a stadium in Soweto he opened his arms to all South Africans: '...no man or woman who has abandoned apartheid will be excluded from our movement towards a non-racial, united and democratic South Africa based on one-person, one-vote on a common voters' roll.'

On 27 February, Mandela attended his first meeting of the National Executive of the ANC, where he was elected deputy president. In the next six months he travelled extensively throughout Africa thanking people for their support and promoting the ANC. Mandela became a hero figure throughout the world and in April 1990 flew to London to be guest of honour at a concert to celebrate his freedom. At the end of the concert Mandela told the jubilant crowd: 'You elected not to forget.... Even through the thickness of the prison walls... we heard your voices demanding our freedom.'

In London, Mandela met the British Prime Minister Margaret Thatcher. Later, when he visited the USA, he met with President George Bush. Mandela spoke of forgiveness and conciliation – in many ways, he already seemed like the president of South Africa. In June 1991 he was elected president of the ANC,

An emotional reunion as ex-prisoners of Robben Island revisit the prison and the quarry at which they worked. Right to left: Wilton Mkwayi, Walter Sisulu, Ahmed Kathrada, Nelson Mandela, Andrew Mlangeni and Dennis Goldberg.

and, in December, the first Convention for a Democratic South Africa (CODESA) was held at the World Trade Center in New York. At these talks Mandela and de Klerk negotiated about the way in which South Africa would be governed in the future. Mandela sought one-person one-vote and majority rule, while de Klerk, who was against majority rule by blacks, insisted on power-sharing.

As the violence in South Africa increased, the negotiatons between Mandela and de Klerk became more heated. Mandela blamed de Klerk for the increasing bloodshed and de Klerk hoped that Mandela would lose his popularity. Despite their differences, an agreement was finally announced in February 1993. They decided upon power-sharing for five years and, from then onwards, majority rule. In June 1993 a date was set for the first national, non-racial, one-person, one-vote election in South Africa – it would go ahead in April 1994. In December 1993, Mandela and de Klerk jointly accepted the Nobel Peace Prize in Norway.

Mandela and de Klerk jointly accept the Nobel Peace Prize of 1993. Behind the scenes, their relationship had by now become frosty.

Different Views

" ... it was a tremendous moment you know. Seeing them coming out hand in hand, so happy with each other. And Nelson just took that huge crowd from whom he had been isolated, for what was it, [27] years with aplomb. I remember that I then appeared the next day on another British TV programme, and they had a psychiatrist there, and the psychiatrist was holding forth, very expansively, about how the truth would suddenly strike Nelson, and he would be totally collapsed by it. They asked me, and I said: 'No, I don't think so. I think he is going to take that in his stride... it's not a false euphoria. This isn't a euphoria at all. It is a real rejoicing. "

Fatima Meer, anti-apartheid activist and friend of Mandela recalling the day of his release. She wrote his authorized biography, Higher Than Hope.

" He said he really was amazed it [the crowd that awaited Mandela on his release] was multi-racial, with so many white people. He really was – well – I mean he was over the moon, but he was also genuinely quite taken aback. "

Archbishop Desmond Tutu.

" Mandela had become such a magical name that the day he was released, everything would be all right, it would all come right. We knew it wasn't going to get fixed in a day, but the expectations were such that this was going to be like the second coming of Christ. "

Journalist Allister Sparks.

A victory salute marks a new beginning: Mandela during the election campaign of 1994.

O N 10 MAY 1994, NELSON MANDELA BECAME the first black president of South Africa. The ANC had won 62.6 per cent of the votes in the general election. F. W. de Klerk, whose National Party had won 20 per cent of the vote, was appointed deputy president. Thabo Mbeki, who would later succeed Mandela as president of South Africa, was also appointed deputy president alongside de Klerk. Mandela's term in office heralded a new era of optimism as he strove to unite the needs of blacks and soothe the fears of whites.

Mandela was realistic about South Africa's transition from an apartheid state to a multi-cultural 'rainbow nation'. He realized that it would take time: 'The policy of apartheid created a deep and lasting wound in my country and people,' he wrote in his autobiography *Long Walk to Freedom*. One of the greatest problems was how to break down the economic divide between blacks and whites. New government policies were introduced to build more houses and improve conditions in health and

education for non-whites. It was now law that black children could join previously all-white schools, but the transition proved difficult for many whites. Parents complained and even went to court to stop black children joining their schools.

While some white people attempted to keep their privileges, many embraced the climate of change. Meanwhile, Mandela went out of his way to make whites feel part of the new South Africa. Grand symbolic gestures, such as meeting Betsie Verwoerd, the widow of Dr Verwoerd, the politician who had introduced so many of the apartheid laws, did much to raise Mandela's profile among whites.

Above the Issue of Race

" He has always been very conscious of people's need to have a community which tends to be their own race, and to belong to that. He has never thought that you would have this idealistic conversion where people don't notice race. At the same time, he's achieved more in terms of multi-racial cooperation than most people thought possible – in his own cabinet, in his own government. And his own lifestyle, where he sometimes doesn't seem to notice what colour anybody is at all…. So that's what appeals to the world so much at the moment, to people like [Tony] Blair or to [Bill] Clinton or to other world leaders is his ability to be above race, not to be a great sort of campaigner or battler, no great anti-racist crusader, which is much less effective. But to somehow appear to be above the whole scene. That's where his life makes such good sense. "

Anthony Sampson, author of the authorized biography of Nelson Mandela, sums up his strengths as president.

Perhaps one of the most poignant moments was when Mandela appeared at the Rugby World Cup Final in 1995 wearing a Springbok jersey. For many years, rugby had been a white-only sport. When Mandela joined the all-white team on the rugby field he earned the love and respect of many Afrikaaners. Mandela's special brand of forgiveness was echoed in the work of the Commission of Truth and Reconciliation. Chaired by Archbishop Desmond Tutu, the commission published a report about apartheid in 1998. For the first time, the victims of apartheid were given a chance to speak about what they had suffered, but they were also encouraged to forgive those who were guilty of crimes against them.

It was always Mandela's intention to retire after serving a five-year term as president. During his time in power his reputation grew throughout the world and hardly anybody had a bad word to say against him. For many reasons, including lack of resources and time, most of the promises laid out by his government were never met. Nevertheless, Mandela's ability to rise above hatred and prejudice had smoothed his country's passage from apartheid state to an all-race democratic nation. When he retired in March 1999, he finally had time to enjoy his own freedom.

South Africa's President Mandela meets with the UK's Princess Diana in May 1997.

In 1992 Mandela and Winnie separated. While Mandela had been in prison, Winnie had become involved in militant politics in Soweto. When she was implicated in the kidnapping and murder of a black boy, Mandela had stood by his wife because he loved her. But upon his release it became evident that they no longer had much in common. Mandela soon found comfort in a new relationship. In 1998, on his eightieth birthday, Mandela married Graca Machel, the widow of President Samora Machel of Mozambique. Mandela and his wife live together in Mandela's birthplace, Qunu, in the Transkei.

At home Mandela looks relaxed and happy as he shares a joke with his third wife, Graca Machel.

Thabo Mbeki with Nelson Mandela during the election campaign of 1999.

WHEN MANDELA STOOD DOWN AS PRESIDENT in 1999 he urged his people to be patient. The South African economy was in poor shape, the promised number of houses had not been built, the crime rates had increased again, and the AIDS epidemic was raging.

Mandela's successor, President Thabo Mbeki has a difficult job following in the footsteps of possibly one of the most popular and charismatic heads of state that has ever been. But he has different qualities to Mandela which stand him in good stead to tackle the economic problems his country faces. He is a quieter and more private man, but he is perhaps better qualified to lead the country. Mbeki is the son of Govan Mbeki, who was imprisoned for life

Mandela's Legacy

"The icon of reconciliation and forgiveness, of holding together a country that everybody kept predicting 'give them six months, and this country will be down the tubes.' It's four years later. I do believe that without him it would not have been possible to hold together those disparate parts that were flying all over the place. That is his greatest legacy.

"And it is a legacy not just for South Africa. When you go round the world now, especially in the aftermath of the Truth and Reconciliation Commission, people do actually look at South Africa and see it as a sign of hope... that will be his greatest achievement apart from having achieved, with all of the people, the liberation of South Africa."

From an interview with Archbishop Desmond Tutu, who was asked how Mandela would be remembered.

alongside Mandela during the Rivonia Trial. Thabo Mbeki played a major role in the ANC throughout the 1970s and 1980s, coordinating anti-apartheid activities at home and abroad.

South Africa today is still recovering after years of apartheid. Many foreign powers no longer invest in the country and the value of the rand (the South African currency) has plummeted. Perhaps the greatest tragedy to hit present-day South Africa is the AIDS epidemic. In 2002, one in nine people in South Africa was HIV positive. AIDS is wiping out an entire generation, leaving behind orphaned children who have no alternative but to fend for themselves. Many of those children also have the HIV virus, while millions of others can only look forward to a life of struggle and poverty. AIDS has had an impact on the economy too – the work force has diminished and industry is struggling to cope.

Thabo Mbeki is not afraid of criticizing the West and of asking for help. In 2002, South Africa hosted the World Summit for Sustainable Development in Johannesburg. In his opening speech, Mbeki called upon the international community to break down the barriers that separate rich and poor throughout the world, and to join together to help the less fortunate.

Nelson Mandela also made an appearance at the 2002 World Summit. Although he has retired from politics, Mandela is often in the news generating support for various charities for children or commenting on world affairs. But when he appeared at the World Summit it was not with his customary smile. This time Mandela was pleading with US President George W. Bush to be cautious about embarking upon a war with Iraq. He accused the USA of threatening world peace. Whether or not people agree with his standpoint, Mandela obviously has an influence in international matters that is unrivalled by other statesmen. Although Mandela now chooses to live his life mainly away from the public eye, the struggle to win freedom for all people remains close to his heart.

By 2010, one in five adults in South Africa is expected to die from AIDS, and life expectancy is predicted to fall from 60 to 40 years.

Glossary

Afrikaaners White South Africans descended from the Dutch colonists who came to South Africa in the seventeenth century.

Afrikaans The language spoken by white South Africans of Dutch descent.

annexed The taking over by one country of part of another country's territory, usually by force.

apartheid A system of segregation, or separation, on the grounds of race.

banned Under apartheid in South Africa a banned person was not allowed to attend meetings of more than one person at a time, appear in public, have his or her speeches mentioned in the media or leave the country. If the person broke the ban he or she could be punished by imprisonment. A banning order was issued by the government to restrain an individual.

Black Power A political movement of black people to obtain equality with whites.

Boers Dutch settlers, or their descendants, living in South Africa from 1652 onwards. By the late eighteenth century, Boers had developed their own language, Afrikaans.

boycott An organized protest where a group of people refuse to have dealings with a person or an organization e.g. by refusing to buy products from a shop or use public transport.

charter A written description of an organization's functions and ideas.

civil rights The rights of individuals to equality and justice.

civil war A war between different groups of people within one country.

colonists People who settle in a country and impose the rules of their own country on that land.

common voters' roll The list of names of people who can vote.

communism A political system under which a country's land, housing and industries belong to the state, and the profits are, in theory, shared among everybody. A follower of communism is known as a communist.

corporal punishment Punishment inflicted on a person's body i.e. by whipping or beating.

democratic Describes a political system where the government is voted for, and is accountable to, its people.

extremist A person who holds extreme political or religious beliefs, and will take extreme action for them.

freedom fighter A person who takes part in violent protest against an established political system or government.

fugitive A person who runs away or hides from the enemy or escapes the law.

guerrilla warfare The planned violence and attacks by members of an independent extreme political group.

homelands The ten territories within South Africa that were formed in the 1970s for black people.

inauguration The ceremony admitting a new president to office.

majority rule Where the party with the majority of votes governs the country.

martial law The suspension of ordinary laws and the military being called in to keep law and order.

maximum security prison A prison with extra security where people considered to be the biggest risk to the general public are imprisoned.

Methodist A member of the Christian Protestant church founded by John and Charles Wesley at Oxford, England, in the eighteenth century.

missionaries People who are sent to a foreign country usually to educate and convert people to their religion.

monopoly The ownership of a service or commodity by one company or nation. This can mean that one company can have full control over how and at what price and to whom a product is sold.

motorcade A procession of motor vehicles.

Nobel Peace Prize An award given each year to the person or organization that has made the greatest contribution to world peace.

passbook An offical document that all non-white South Africans had to carry at all times during apartheid. No black person was allowed to remain in a white area for longer than 72 hours unless he or she had special permission.

passive resistance Peaceful demonstration, or non-violent resistance, against a government or law.

pass laws The series of laws about where people of different races were allowed to go, passed by the South African government during apartheid.

race laws Any laws that are passed to control the lives of people based upon their ethnic background.

racial segregation The separation of different racial groups.

reconciliation The act of being friendly or compatible with somebody after having been enemies.

Secretary General The most senior administrator of an organization or government.

secret service A network of spies or underground police operating in secret on behalf of the government.

solidarity Unity or agreement among people or organizations to act together.

State of Emergency A period of time in which the government of a country employs the army and arrests political opponents, in order to remain in power.

stay-at-home A type of organized political protest in which masses of people do not go to work, use public services or attend shops for a set period of time.

Thembu The people from Thembuland, the southern part of the Transkei in South Africa. Nelson Mandela belongs to this group of people.

township A small town or area of a South African town or city that has been set aside for black housing.

trade sanctions Measures taken against a country by other countries to force a change of policy. From the 1970s, many countries organized boycotts of South African goods.

underground The hidden or secret activity of a political group that aims to topple the existing government.

United Nations (UN) An organization established in October 1945 to work for world peace, which now has representatives from most of the world's nations.

UN Security Council The arm of the UN responsible for maintaining peace and stability in the world. In times of political unrest or possible war, it can call upon UN members to take military or economic action.

white extremist groups Violent, all-white political groups that formed in South Africa in opposition to the lifting of apartheid and the election of an all-black government.

white supremacy The theory that white people are superior to people of other races.

Xhosa Bantu-speaking people who make up the second-largest ethnic group in South Africa. Nelson Mandela is proud of his Xhosa heritage.

Zulu Bantu-speaking people who make up the largest ethnic group in South Africa. Historically, the Zulus controlled a powerful military empire.

Further Information

Reading

The End of Apartheid by Catherine Bradley (Evans Brothers, 1995)

11 February 1990: The Release of Nelson Mandela by John Malam (Cherrytree Books, 2002)

Famous Lives: Nelson Mandela by Hakim Adi (Hodder Wayland, 2000)

Leading Lives: Nelson Mandela by Liz Gogerly (Heinemann, 2002)

Profiles: Nelson Mandela by Sean Connolly (Heinemann, 2001)

The Story of Nelson Mandela by James Riordan and Neil Reed (Belitha Press, 2001)

Lives in Crisis: South Africa Since Apartheid by Sean Sheehan (Hodder Wayland, 2002)

Films

Cry the Beloved Country directed by Darrell James Roodt, 1995

Cry Freedom directed by Richard Attenborough, 1987

Sarafina directed by Darrell James Roodt, 1998

Timeline

1910 The Union of South Africa is formed.

1912 South African Native National Congress is formed.

1913 The Natives Land Act is passed.

18 July 1918 Nelson Mandela is born in the Transkei.

1944 Nelson Mandela, Oliver Tambo and Walter Sisulu form the ANC Youth League.

1948 Dr Daniel Malan is elected prime minister of South Africa and introduces apartheid.

1949 The Prohibition of Mixed Marriages Act is passed.

1950 The Population Registration Act, the Suppression of Communism Act and the Group Areas Act are passed. Mandela made president of the ANC Youth League.

1952 Mandela sets up the first black law firm in South Africa with Oliver Tambo; Mandela draws up the M-Plan.

26 June 1952 Start of the Defiance Campaign.

1956 Mandela is arrested, the Treason Trial begins.

June 1958 Mandela marries Winnie Madikizela.

1959 University segregation is imposed, the Pan Africanist Congress (PAC) is formed.

1960 ANC is banned; Sharpeville massacre takes place.

1961 Umkhonto we Sizwe (MK) is launched. South Africa leaves the British Commonwealth.

1962 The Sabotage Act, General Laws Amendment Act and other laws are passed. Mandela is arrested and jailed for five years at Robben Island.

11 July 1963 Mandela faces charges of high treason.

1964 ANC leaders, including Mandela, are jailed for life.

1967 The ANC begins guerrilla warfare.

1969 The South African Students' Organization is founded.

1972 The Black People's Convention is formed.

1975 Inkatha, a Zulu cultural organization is re-formed.

1976 The Soweto schoolchildren uprising takes place.

1977 Steve Biko is killed while in police detention.

1978 P. W. Botha replaces Vorster as prime minister.

1980 Protests, strikes and school boycotts in South Africa.

1982 Mandela is transferred to Pollsmoor prison.

1984 New constitution comes into effect; P. W. Botha becomes executive president.

1985 Declaration of a State of Emergency.

1986 State of Emergency lifted.

1988 Mandela is transferred to Victor Verster prison and begins private meetings with the government.

1989 P. W. Botha resigns; de Klerk takes power.

1990 F. W. de Klerk unbans ANC, PAC and South African Communist Party; Mandela is released from prison; violence erupts in Natal; ANC and South African government meet; ANC suspends armed struggle.

1991 A National Peace Accord is signed; Mandela is elected president of the ANC; Convention for a Democratic South Africa (CODESA) begins talks.

1992 CODESA talks halt; ANC withdraws from CODESA.

1993 Mandela and de Klerk receive Nobel Peace Prize.

1994 South Africa's first all-race democratic elections take place; Mandela becomes president of South Africa.

March 1996 Mandela divorces Winnie; South Africa adopts a new constitution which includes a bill of rights guaranteeing equality for all its peoples.

December 1997 Mandela steps down as ANC president.

18 July 1998 Mandela marries Graca Machel on his eightieth birthday.

February 1999 Mandela's final opening of Parliament; Mandela steps down as president.